1000 NATURAL DISASTERS

Coyright © 2024

All rights reserved. No part of this publication may be reproduced, distributed, or transmitted in any form or by any means, including photocopying, recording, or other electronic or mechanical methods, without the prior written permission of the publisher, except in the case of brief quotations embodied in critical reviews and certain other noncommercial uses permitted by copyright law.

Table of Content

Earthquakes 5
Volcanoes............................14
Tsunamis.............................23
Tornadoes...........................32
Floods................................41
Storms 50
Blizzards.............................56
Wildfires 65
Heatwaves.........................74
Hurricanes..........................83
Landslides..........................92
Natural Disasters in History........101

Natural disasters like earthquakes, tsunamis, and hurricanes show the power of nature. This collection highlights some of the most impactful events in history and their effects on people and the planet.

EARTHQUAKES

- Earthquakes are caused by sudden movements in the Earth's crust.
- The Earth's crust is made up of large pieces called tectonic plates.
- Tectonic plates float on a layer of molten rock called the mantle.
- When tectonic plates collide, pull apart, or slide past each other, earthquakes occur.
- The place where an earthquake starts is called the focus.
- The point directly above the focus on the Earth's surface is called the epicenter.
- Earthquakes can happen under the land or the ocean.
- When an earthquake occurs underwater, it can cause a tsunami.
- Scientists who study earthquakes are called seismologists.
- Seismologists use a tool called a

seismograph to measure earthquakes.
- The strength of an earthquake is measured on a scale called the Richter scale.
- Earthquakes are also described by their intensity using the Mercalli scale.
- Small earthquakes that happen after a big one are called aftershocks.
- Earthquakes can last for just a few seconds or several minutes.
- The Earth's strongest earthquakes often occur near tectonic plate boundaries.
- The largest recorded earthquake was in Chile in 1960, measuring 9.5 on the Richter scale.
- Japan experiences many earthquakes because it is located on the Ring of Fire.
- The Ring of Fire is a horseshoe-shaped area with lots of volcanic and earthquake activity.
- California is known for earthquakes

because of the San Andreas Fault.
- A fault is a crack in the Earth's crust where movement happens.
- The shaking during an earthquake is called seismic waves.
- Seismic waves move through the Earth like ripples in water.
- There are three types of seismic waves: P-waves, S-waves, and surface waves.
- P-waves are the fastest and move through both solids and liquids.
- S-waves are slower and move only through solids.
- Surface waves travel along the Earth's surface and cause the most damage.
- Some earthquakes are so small that they cannot be felt by people.
- Earthquakes below magnitude 2.0 are called microquakes.

- Major earthquakes, over magnitude 7.0, can cause serious destruction.
- Earthquakes can make buildings, bridges, and roads collapse.
- Engineers design earthquake-resistant buildings to reduce damage.
- Some animals might sense earthquakes before humans do.
- Earthquakes can cause landslides and rockfalls in mountains.
- A large earthquake can even change the shape of the land.
- In 2011, an earthquake in Japan moved the island of Honshu by 8 feet.
- Earthquakes can create cracks in the ground called fissures.
- Some earthquakes occur in places with no tectonic plates, called intraplate earthquakes.

- The largest intraplate earthquake in the U.S. was the New Madrid Earthquake in 1811-1812.
- Liquefaction occurs when soil turns into a liquid during an earthquake.
- Earthquakes can also break gas pipes and start fires.
- The Dead Sea in the Middle East is sinking due to tectonic plate movement.
- Many ancient cities were destroyed by earthquakes.
- An earthquake destroyed the city of Pompeii before it was buried by a volcano.
- The Himalayas are still rising because of tectonic plate movement.
- Earthquakes on the moon are called moonquakes.
- Moonquakes are much weaker than earthquakes on Earth.

- Mars also has quakes, called marsquakes.
- Earthquakes can happen at any time of the day or night.
- Earthquake drills help people know what to do during an earthquake.
- The best way to stay safe is to "Drop, Cover, and Hold On".
- Most earthquakes happen less than 50 miles below the Earth's surface.
- Deep-focus earthquakes can occur as far as 400 miles below the surface.
- Earthquakes can happen in Antarctica too, but they are rare.
- Some earthquakes are caused by human activities, like mining or building dams.
- Earthquakes help scientists understand the inside of the Earth.
- The deepest earthquake ever recorded occurred 609 kilometers (378 miles) below

the Earth's surface.
- Earthquakes can trigger avalanches in snowy areas.
- The first recorded earthquake dates back to 1177 BCE in China.
- Earthquakes can create new hot springs by shifting underground water.
- A seismometer can detect earthquakes that are too small for humans to feel.
- Some regions have earthquake early warning systems to save lives.
- Earthquake-proof furniture can prevent injuries indoors.
- Trees and plants near fault lines can shift over time due to earthquakes.
- Ancient people thought earthquakes were caused by angry gods or giant animals.
- Earthquakes happen more often in some places, called seismic zones.

- Earthquakes can be followed by other natural disasters like tsunamis or volcanic eruptions.
- Indonesia has one of the highest earthquake risks in the world.
- In 2004, an earthquake in the Indian Ocean caused a tsunami that killed over 200,000 people.
- Earthquakes cannot be predicted, but scientists can estimate their likelihood.
- Earthquakes can release as much energy as thousands of nuclear bombs.
- Scientists are studying ways to use small earthquakes to release pressure and prevent big ones.
- The Earth's crust is constantly moving, even when there are no earthquakes.

VOLCANO

- A volcano is an opening in the Earth's surface where magma escapes.
- Magma is molten rock beneath the Earth's surface.
- When magma reaches the surface, it is called lava.
- Volcanoes can erupt with lava, ash, and gases.
- Volcanoes are usually found at the edges of tectonic plates.
- There are three types of volcanoes: shield, cinder cone, and composite.
- Shield volcanoes have gentle slopes and erupt lava gently.
- Cinder cone volcanoes are small and erupt explosively.
- Composite volcanoes are tall and erupt violently.

- The largest volcano on Earth is Mauna Loa in Hawaii.
- The tallest volcano in the solar system is Olympus Mons on Mars.
- A volcano can be active, dormant, or extinct.
- Active volcanoes erupt regularly.
- Dormant volcanoes haven't erupted for a long time but could erupt again.
- Extinct volcanoes are not expected to erupt again.
- The Ring of Fire is home to 75% of the world's volcanoes.
- The Ring of Fire is a circle of volcanoes around the Pacific Ocean.
- Lava can be as hot as 1,250°C (2,282°F).
- Volcanic ash can travel hundreds of miles from the eruption.

- A volcano's eruption can create new islands.
- Iceland was formed by volcanic eruptions.
- Hawaii is made up of volcanoes, including Mauna Kea and Kilauea.
- Mount Vesuvius buried the city of Pompeii in AD 79.
- Volcanoes can cause earthquakes during eruptions.
- Hot lava cools to form new rocks.
- A volcanic crater is the bowl-shaped opening at the top of a volcano.
- A caldera is a large crater formed when a volcano collapses.
- Volcanic eruptions release gases like carbon dioxide and sulfur dioxide.
- Volcanic eruptions can cause global cooling by blocking sunlight.

- Volcanoes create fertile soil that helps plants grow.
- Geysers, like Old Faithful, are caused by volcanic heat.
- Volcanoes can erupt underwater, creating seamounts.
- The deepest underwater volcano is West Mata, in the Pacific Ocean.
- Lava tubes are tunnels formed by flowing lava.
- Some volcanoes erupt explosively, while others ooze lava slowly.
- Pyroclastic flows are fast-moving clouds of hot gas and ash.
- Lahar is a dangerous volcanic mudflow.
- Pumice is a light volcanic rock that can float on water.
- The loudest sound in recorded history was

from the Krakatoa eruption in 1883.
- Supervolcanoes can erupt with enormous amounts of ash and lava.
- Yellowstone National Park sits on a supervolcano.
- A supervolcanic eruption could affect the entire planet.
- Volcanoes have been erupting for billions of years.
- Ancient people thought volcanoes were homes of gods.
- The word "volcano" comes from Vulcan, the Roman god of fire.
- Volcanoes are monitored with tools like seismographs and satellites.
- Scientists who study volcanoes are called volcanologists.
- Volcanic eruptions can create lightning in

the ash cloud.

• Lava can flow at speeds up to 6 miles per hour.

• Volcanic eruptions can last from minutes to years.

• Some volcanoes release lava fountains hundreds of feet high.

• Lava domes are formed by slow eruptions of thick lava.

• Some animals, like the Galápagos finches, live near volcanoes.

• The Parícutin volcano in Mexico erupted in a farmer's field in 1943.

• Volcanic eruptions can create lakes in craters.

• Lake Toba in Indonesia is a supervolcano caldera.

• Black sand beaches are made from volcanic

rock.
- **Volcanic activity can form hot springs and natural steam vents.**
- **Many gemstones, like obsidian, come from volcanic rock.**
- **Lava flows can destroy everything in their path.**
- **Volcanic eruptions under glaciers can cause massive floods.**
- **Underwater volcanoes create hydrothermal vents that support unique sea life.**
- **Volcanic eruptions on Earth helped create the atmosphere.**
- **Volcanoes can be as small as a hill or as large as a mountain.**
- **The Pacific Plate has the most volcanoes.**
- **Some volcanoes erupt every few years, while others erupt every 100,000 years.**

- **Volcanoes can also release steam and hot gases without lava.**
- **Active volcanoes can be found on every continent, even Antarctica.**
- **Mount Etna in Italy is one of the most active volcanoes in the world.**
- **Volcanoes are natural reminders of the Earth's power and energy!**

TSUNAMIS

- A tsunami is a series of huge ocean waves caused by underwater events.
- The word "tsunami" comes from the Japanese words "tsu" (harbor) and "nami" (wave).
- Tsunamis are usually caused by underwater earthquakes.
- Other causes of tsunamis include volcanic eruptions, landslides, and meteor impacts.
- Most tsunamis are caused by earthquakes near tectonic plate boundaries.
- The sudden movement of the seafloor displaces water, creating a tsunami.
- Tsunamis are not like regular waves caused by the wind.
- In deep water, tsunami waves travel very fast but are not very tall.
- Tsunamis can travel as fast as a jet

plane—up to 500 miles per hour!
- As a tsunami approaches shallow water near land, it slows down and grows taller.
- Tsunami waves can reach heights of over 100 feet (30 meters).
- A series of tsunami waves is called a "wave train."
- The first tsunami wave is often not the largest.
- Tsunamis can cause flooding and destroy buildings near the coast.
- Tsunamis can travel thousands of miles across the ocean.
- People on the other side of the ocean can be affected hours later.
- The 2004 Indian Ocean tsunami was one of the deadliest, killing over 230,000 people.
- The 2011 Japan tsunami caused massive

destruction and nuclear plant damage.

• A tsunami warning system can help save lives.

• Tsunami warning systems use sensors on the ocean floor to detect changes in water pressure.

• If you feel an earthquake near the coast, it could mean a tsunami is coming.

• A sudden retreat of water from the shoreline is a warning sign of a tsunami.

• Tsunamis can hit within minutes of an earthquake or hours later.

• Coastal areas with steep slopes are more vulnerable to tsunamis.

• Islands can protect the mainland by slowing down tsunami waves.

• Tsunamis can carry debris like cars, trees, and boats far inland.

- The Pacific Ocean is the most common area for tsunamis, especially along the Ring of Fire.
- The largest tsunami ever recorded was in Alaska in 1958, reaching 1,720 feet high.
- That tsunami was caused by a massive landslide into a bay.
- Tsunamis can occur in any ocean or large body of water.
- Even lakes can experience tsunamis, often caused by landslides.
- Tsunamis can be detected hours before they reach land.
- Some animals, like elephants, can sense tsunamis before they happen.
- Coastal mangroves and coral reefs can help reduce tsunami impact.
- People living in tsunami-prone areas should

have an evacuation plan.
- Tsunami drills teach people how to stay safe during an event.
- A "tsunami watch" means a tsunami might happen, while a "tsunami warning" means one is on the way.
- Boats in deep water are safer during a tsunami than those near shore.
- Tsunami waves are very long, sometimes stretching for hundreds of miles.
- The energy of a tsunami can move across the entire ocean.
- The energy of a tsunami comes from the movement of tectonic plates.
- A tsunami's energy can weaken as it travels farther from its source.
- Tsunamis can cause massive erosion, reshaping coastlines.

- **Tsunamis have been recorded in history for thousands of years.**
- **Ancient Greek historians wrote about tsunamis in the Mediterranean.**
- **A tsunami destroyed the ancient city of Helike in Greece in 373 BC.**
- **The Atlantic Ocean also has tsunamis, but they are less frequent.**
- **The Canary Islands could trigger a tsunami in the Atlantic if a landslide occurs.**
- **Some people call tsunamis "tidal waves," but they are not related to tides.**
- **Tsunamis can move entire buildings from one place to another.**
- **Volcanic eruptions, like Krakatoa in 1883, can create deadly tsunamis.**
- **Tsunamis can create strong currents that pull people and objects out to sea.**

- The shape of the coastline affects how tsunamis behave when they reach land.
- Coastal areas with wide, shallow bays are more vulnerable to tsunamis.
- Tsunamis can destroy ports and harbors, affecting trade and fishing.
- Coastal warning sirens alert people to evacuate in case of a tsunami.
- High ground is the safest place to be during a tsunami.
- A small earthquake offshore doesn't always mean a tsunami will follow.
- Tsunamis can also happen without any noticeable earthquake.
- Scientists use computer models to predict how tsunamis will spread.
- Evacuation routes in tsunami-prone areas are marked with signs.

- Tsunamis can knock out power and communication systems.
- Some people survive tsunamis by climbing trees or tall buildings.
- Tsunamis can happen day or night, making preparedness important.
- Coastal communities often build sea walls to block tsunami waves.
- Countries around the Pacific Ocean work together in a warning network.
- After a tsunami, cleanup and rebuilding can take years.
- Tsunamis remind us of the power of nature and the need to stay prepared.
- Learning about tsunamis can help kids stay safe and informed.

TORNADOES

A tornado is a spinning column of air that touches both the ground and a cloud.
- Tornadoes are also called twisters or cyclones.
- Tornadoes form during severe thunderstorms.
- The most violent tornadoes can reach wind speeds over 300 miles per hour.
- Tornadoes are created by a rotating storm called a supercell.
- Supercells are thunderstorms with a strong, rotating updraft of air.
- Tornadoes are shaped like funnels or ropes.
- The part of the tornado visible to us is made of dust and debris.
- Tornadoes are measured using the Enhanced Fujita (EF) Scale.

- The EF Scale rates tornadoes from EF0 (weak) to EF5 (extreme).
- EF0 tornadoes have winds of 65–85 mph and cause minor damage.
- EF5 tornadoes have winds over 200 mph and can destroy entire buildings.
- Tornadoes can last from a few seconds to over an hour.
- The average tornado lasts about 10 minutes.
- The United States experiences more tornadoes than any other country.
- Tornado Alley is a region in the U.S. with frequent tornadoes.
- Tornado Alley includes parts of Texas, Oklahoma, Kansas, and Nebraska.
- Tornadoes can also occur in other parts of the world, like Canada and Europe.

- Tornadoes in the Southern Hemisphere rotate clockwise.
- In the Northern Hemisphere, tornadoes rotate counterclockwise.
- A tornado forms when warm, moist air meets cold, dry air.
- Tornadoes are most common in spring and summer.
- Tornadoes can happen at any time of the day or night.
- Tornadoes are most likely to occur in the late afternoon or early evening.
- Tornadoes can travel across land at speeds up to 60 miles per hour.
- The fastest-moving tornado traveled at 73 mph in 1925.
- Tornadoes can lift cars, animals, and even houses into the air.

- A tornado's path can be as short as a few feet or as long as 50 miles.
- The widest tornado ever recorded was 2.6 miles wide in El Reno, Oklahoma, in 2013.
- Tornadoes can occur over water, and they are called waterspouts.
- Waterspouts are usually weaker than land tornadoes.
- Tornadoes that form in deserts are called dust devils.
- Tornadoes can produce loud roaring noises, like a freight train.
- A tornado watch means conditions are right for a tornado to form.
- A tornado warning means a tornado has been spotted or detected.
- Tornadoes can form very quickly, sometimes with little warning.

- Radar systems help meteorologists detect tornadoes.
- Doppler radar can measure the rotation of storms that create tornadoes.
- Tornado sirens are used to warn people to take shelter.
- The safest place during a tornado is a basement or storm shelter.
- If you don't have a basement, go to an interior room without windows.
- Mobile homes are especially vulnerable to tornadoes.
- Tornadoes can rip trees out of the ground and carry them far away.
- Some tornadoes throw objects hundreds of feet into the air.
- Tornadoes can pick up fish or frogs and drop them in strange places.

- A tornado in Kansas in 1928 dropped thousands of frogs!
- Tornado outbreaks are groups of tornadoes happening in one region.
- The largest tornado outbreak in the U.S. was in 2011, with 360 tornadoes in 3 days.
- The deadliest tornado in U.S. history occurred in 1925, killing 695 people.
- The strongest tornado ever recorded happened in Oklahoma in 1999 with winds of 318 mph.
- Tornadoes can uproot entire forests in seconds.
- Tornadoes can cause "suction spots," areas of intense upward wind.
- Some animals, like dogs, may sense tornadoes before they happen.
- Tornadoes can destroy entire towns but

leave some buildings untouched.
- Tornadoes can strip the bark off trees.
- Tornadoes are often accompanied by hail, heavy rain, and lightning.
- Tornadoes can happen during hurricanes when the storm makes landfall.
- The average tornado is about 660 feet wide.
- Tornado debris can travel hundreds of miles.
- Tornadoes are often preceded by a greenish sky.
- Storm chasers are people who study tornadoes up close.
- Scientists study tornadoes to improve forecasting and save lives.
- Tornado shelters are specially designed to withstand high winds.

- The first recorded tornado in history happened in Ireland in 1054.
- Tornadoes on other planets, like Jupiter, are called whirlwinds.
- Tornado drills teach kids what to do during a storm.
- Tornadoes remind us of the power and unpredictability of nature.
- Staying informed and prepared is the best way to stay safe during a tornado.
- Learning about tornadoes helps us understand how our planet works.

FLOODS

- A flood happens when water covers land that is usually dry.
- Floods can be caused by heavy rain, melting snow, or overflowing rivers.
- Coastal floods are caused by high tides, storm surges, or tsunamis.
- Flash floods happen very quickly and with little warning.
- Flash floods are often caused by heavy rainfall in a short time.
- River floods occur when rivers overflow their banks.
- Urban floods happen when cities can't drain rainwater quickly enough.
- Floods are one of the most common natural disasters in the world.
- Floods can happen anywhere, even in deserts.

- Flooding is more likely in areas with flat land or near rivers.
- Hurricanes and tropical storms can cause coastal flooding.
- Ice jams in rivers can cause flooding when ice blocks water flow.
- Dams and levees can fail, causing sudden floods.
- Snowmelt floods happen when warm temperatures melt snow quickly.
- Floods can carry mud, debris, and even large objects.
- Floodwaters can rise slowly or very quickly, depending on the type of flood.
- The deadliest flood in history occurred in China in 1931, killing millions.
- Floods can destroy homes, roads, and bridges.

- Flooding can cause landslides in hilly or mountainous areas.
- The force of floodwater can move cars and uproot trees.
- Floods can contaminate drinking water, making it unsafe to drink.
- Floodwater often carries harmful bacteria and chemicals.
- Animals and plants can be displaced by floods.
- Floods can destroy crops, leading to food shortages.
- Wetlands, like marshes, can help absorb floodwaters.
- Floodplains are areas of land that flood regularly.
- People often build levees and dams to prevent flooding.

- Floods can happen quickly during storms or take days to develop.
- Some animals, like frogs, thrive after floods due to extra water.
- Floods can create lakes in low-lying areas.
- Flash floods are the leading cause of weather-related deaths in the U.S.
- Flood warnings help people prepare and evacuate when needed.
- Floods are more common during rainy seasons or monsoons.
- Floods can occur when tropical storms push ocean water onto land.
- Rising sea levels due to climate change increase the risk of flooding.
- Some deserts experience flash floods after rare rainstorms.
- Floods can erode soil and reshape the land.

- Floods can spread seeds and help plants grow in new areas.
- Ancient civilizations, like those in Mesopotamia, relied on floodwaters for farming.
- The annual flooding of the Nile River helped ancient Egyptians grow crops.
- Beavers build dams that can cause small-scale flooding.
- Heavy rainfall in cities can cause urban flooding due to poor drainage.
- Floods can knock down power lines and cause blackouts.
- During floods, people are advised to evacuate to higher ground.
- Some floods are caused by natural disasters like earthquakes and tsunamis.
- Flood insurance helps people recover after

a flood damages their property.

• Sandbags are used to block water and protect buildings during floods.

• Droughts can follow floods, creating extreme weather patterns.

• Floods can damage historical sites and artifacts.

• Animals like alligators and snakes may appear in floodwaters.

• Floods can create temporary habitats for fish and water birds.

• People living in flood-prone areas should have an emergency plan.

• Floodwater can be very strong, even at shallow depths.

• Six inches of moving water can knock a person off their feet.

• Two feet of water can sweep away a car.

- After a flood, it's important to clean homes to prevent mold.
- Floodwaters can destroy roads, making it hard for emergency workers to help.
- Plants can regrow in areas where floods leave nutrient-rich soil.
- Floods can refill dried-up lakes and wetlands.
- Floods are sometimes caused by climate events like El Niño.
- Global warming is making floods more frequent in some areas.
- Flood sirens warn people to leave areas at risk.
- Building homes on stilts can protect against floods in flood-prone areas.
- Early warning systems and weather forecasts help prevent flood damage.

- In some places, seasonal flooding is part of life and farming cycles.
- Floods can wash away animals' homes, forcing them to move.
- Mangrove forests protect coastlines from floods and storm surges.
- Flooding can damage underground water pipes and septic systems.
- People often rebuild communities in flood-prone areas after disasters.
- Floods can remind us of the power of nature and the importance of preparedness.

STORMS

- A storm is a violent weather event with strong winds, rain, thunder, or snow.
- Thunderstorms are the most common type of storm.
- Thunderstorms form when warm, moist air rises and cools quickly.
- Thunderstorms can produce heavy rain, hail, and lightning.
- Lightning is a giant spark of electricity in the atmosphere.
- A bolt of lightning can heat the air to 30,000°C (54,000°F).
- Thunder is the sound caused by lightning heating the air.
- You see lightning before you hear thunder because light travels faster than sound.
- Hail is frozen raindrops that grow larger in strong thunderstorms.

- Tornadoes can form during severe thunderstorms.
- Storms are more common during spring and summer.
- Hurricanes, typhoons, and cyclones are all names for the same type of storm.
- Hurricanes form over warm ocean waters near the equator.
- A hurricane's center is called the eye, where it is calm.
- The strongest winds and heaviest rain in a hurricane occur in the eye wall.
- Hurricanes are measured on the Saffir-Simpson scale, from Category 1 to 5.
- Tropical storms are weaker than hurricanes but still very dangerous.
- A storm surge is a rise in sea level caused by a hurricane's winds.

- Blizzards are winter storms with heavy snow and strong winds.
- A snowstorm becomes a blizzard when visibility is very low for at least 3 hours.
- Ice storms occur when rain freezes as it hits cold surfaces.
- Dust storms happen in dry, windy areas and can last for hours.
- Sandstorms occur in deserts and can bury roads and buildings in sand.
- Windstorms can happen even without rain or snow.
- The strongest winds ever recorded in a storm were 254 mph in a tropical cyclone in Australia.
- Storm clouds are called cumulonimbus clouds.
- Storms can produce updrafts and

downdrafts of wind.

• A microburst is a small, powerful downdraft of wind from a storm.

• Thunderstorms can happen in any season, even winter.

• Heat lightning is lightning you see from a storm far away.

• A derecho is a long-lasting storm with powerful straight-line winds.

• Supercell storms are the strongest type of thunderstorm.

• Supercells can produce tornadoes, hail, and heavy rain.

• A storm watch means conditions are right for a storm to form.

• A storm warning means a storm is happening or about to happen.

• People can stay safe during storms by

taking shelter indoors.
• Lightning can strike the same place more than once.
• Trees and tall buildings are more likely to be struck by lightning.
• A lightning rod can protect buildings from lightning damage.
• Storms can knock down power lines, causing blackouts.
• Storms can uproot trees and damage homes.
• Flooding is a common effect of storms with heavy rain.
• Hailstones can grow as big as softballs in strong storms.
• Storms can create rainbows when sunlight passes through raindrops.
• Thunderstorms can trigger landslides in

BLIZZARDS

- A blizzard is a severe snowstorm with strong winds and low visibility.
- For a storm to be called a blizzard, winds must be at least 35 mph.
- Blizzards last for at least three hours with heavy snow or blowing snow.
- During a blizzard, visibility is reduced to less than a quarter mile.
- Blizzards can happen in areas with cold temperatures and moisture.
- The U.S. Midwest and Northeast often experience blizzards.
- A blizzard in the mountains is called a whiteout because you can't see anything.
- Blizzards are more common in winter but can happen in early spring or late fall.
- The combination of snow and wind makes blizzards dangerous.

- Blizzards can create snow drifts, which are piles of snow blown by the wind.
- Snow drifts during a blizzard can be taller than a house!
- Blizzards can knock out power and block roads with snow.
- Temperatures during a blizzard can feel much colder due to wind chill.
- Wind chill is how cold it feels when wind blows on your skin.
- Frostbite can occur during a blizzard if skin is exposed for too long.
- Hypothermia is a danger during blizzards if you get too cold.
- People should stay indoors during blizzards to stay safe and warm.
- If caught outside in a blizzard, find shelter and stay dry.

- Blizzards can trap people in their homes for days.
- Snowplows work to clear roads during and after blizzards.
- A blizzard can dump several feet of snow in one area.
- After a blizzard, roads and sidewalks can become icy and slippery.
- Schools and businesses often close during a blizzard for safety.
- Blizzards can delay flights and shut down airports.
- Animals may struggle to find food during blizzards because of the deep snow.
- Some animals, like bears, hibernate during the winter to avoid blizzards.
- Birds often fly to warmer areas before a blizzard strikes.

- Blizzards can cause snow blindness, a temporary condition caused by sunlight reflecting off snow.
- Snow goggles can protect eyes during a blizzard.
- Blizzards can damage trees by weighing down branches with snow.
- A ground blizzard happens when strong winds blow existing snow without new snowfall.
- The Great Blizzard of 1888 was one of the worst in U.S. history.
- The 1888 blizzard dropped 50 inches of snow and caused massive snow drifts.
- Antarctica experiences frequent blizzards because of its cold and windy climate.
- The coldest blizzards occur in the Arctic and Antarctic regions.

- Blizzards can make outdoor travel dangerous due to poor visibility.
- Snowmobiles are sometimes used to travel during blizzards.
- People prepare for blizzards by stocking up on food, water, and supplies.
- A blizzard warning is issued when a blizzard is expected within 24 hours.
- A winter storm watch means conditions are right for a blizzard to form.
- Blizzards can bury cars and make them difficult to find.
- Icicles often form on buildings during and after blizzards.
- Blizzards can freeze rivers, lakes, and ponds, making them safe for ice skating.
- Polar bears thrive in blizzard conditions in the Arctic.

- A warm coat, gloves, and boots are essential during a blizzard.
- Homes need proper insulation to stay warm during blizzards.
- Blizzards can cause roofs to collapse under the weight of heavy snow.
- Emergency shelters may open for people without heat during blizzards.
- Blizzards often follow strong cold fronts.
- A Nor'easter is a type of storm that brings blizzards to the U.S. East Coast.
- Nor'easters get their name from the strong northeastern winds they bring.
- Snow during a blizzard can be light and fluffy or heavy and wet.
- Wet snow is heavier and harder to shovel after a blizzard.
- Blizzards can delay mail delivery and dis-

rupt communication.

• Kids love playing in the snow after a blizzard ends!

• Sledding, snowball fights, and building snow forts are fun activities after a blizzard.

• Blizzards are part of the Earth's natural weather cycle.

• Snow during a blizzard helps insulate the ground and protect plants.

• Farmers rely on snowmelt after a blizzard to water crops in the spring.

• Blizzards can be beautiful, with snow-covered landscapes glittering in the sun.

• People use snowshoes to walk on deep snow after a blizzard.

• Dogs like huskies and malamutes are bred to thrive in snowy conditions.

• Blizzards can cause avalanches in mountainous areas.

• Weather satellites help meteorologists predict blizzards.

• Some blizzards are so strong that they are remembered for decades.

• Learning about blizzards helps people stay safe during winter storms.

• Blizzards remind us of the power and beauty of nature!

WILDFIRES

- **A wildfire is an uncontrolled fire that burns in forests, grasslands, or other natural areas.**
- **Wildfires can spread quickly, fueled by wind, heat, and dry vegetation.**
- **Wildfires are also called forest fires, bushfires, or grassfires, depending on where they occur.**
- **Wildfires can start naturally or be caused by humans.**
- **Lightning is one of the most common natural causes of wildfires.**
- **Human activities, like campfires, fireworks, or discarded cigarettes, can start wildfires.**
- **Wildfires need three things to burn: heat, fuel, and oxygen.**
- **Dry plants, like grass and leaves, are the fuel for wildfires.**

- Wildfires can happen anywhere but are most common in dry, hot areas.
- The United States, Australia, and Canada experience many wildfires.
- Wildfires are most common during the summer and fall.
- Strong winds can make wildfires spread faster.
- Wildfires can travel at speeds up to 14 miles per hour.
- Some wildfires are small, but others can burn thousands of acres.
- Wildfires can destroy homes, trees, and wildlife habitats.
- Animals often flee wildfires, but some hide underground or in water.
- Firefighters work hard to put out wildfires and protect people.

- Special planes and helicopters drop water or fire retardant to fight wildfires.
- Firebreaks are gaps in vegetation that help stop wildfires from spreading.
- Wildfires can produce huge clouds of smoke that travel long distances.
- Smoke from wildfires can affect air quality, even in areas far away.
- Wildfires can create their own weather, including fire tornadoes.
- Fire tornadoes, or fire whirls, are spinning columns of fire and smoke.
- Wildfires are sometimes started on purpose to prevent larger fires.
- Controlled burns remove dry vegetation to reduce the risk of wildfires.
- Wildfires are part of nature's cycle and can help forests grow back stronger.

- Some trees, like pine trees, release seeds during wildfires.
- Wildfires clear out old plants, making space for new growth.
- After a wildfire, flowers and grasses often grow back quickly.
- Animals return to burned areas once new plants grow.
- The largest wildfire in U.S. history burned 3 million acres in 1910.
- Wildfires can cause landslides by burning away plants that hold soil in place.
- People in wildfire-prone areas use fire-resistant materials to build homes.
- Wildfire warnings help people prepare and evacuate if needed.
- A red flag warning means conditions are right for wildfires to start.

- Wildfires can burn underground in peat bogs for months or even years.
- The world's longest-burning fire has been burning underground in Australia for 6,000 years!
- Wildfires can destroy entire towns but spare some buildings.
- Firefighters wear special suits and masks to protect themselves from heat and smoke.
- Smokejumpers are firefighters who parachute into remote areas to fight wildfires.
- Drones and satellites are used to track and monitor wildfires.
- Wildfires can jump across rivers and roads if sparks travel on the wind.
- Some animals, like birds of prey, use wildfires to hunt smaller animals.

- **Koalas and other animals may be rescued from wildfires and cared for by humans.**
- **Wildfires are becoming more frequent due to climate change.**
- **Rising temperatures and droughts make forests drier and more flammable.**
- **Wildfires can harm water supplies by filling rivers with ash and debris.**
- **Forests that burn too often may not recover fully.**
- **Wildfires can leave behind blackened, charred land called burn scars.**
- **Wildfires release carbon dioxide into the atmosphere, affecting the climate.**
- **People can help prevent wildfires by being careful with fire outdoors.**
- **Never leave a campfire unattended to avoid starting a wildfire.**

- **Smokey Bear reminds people that "Only YOU can prevent wildfires."**
- **Wildfires can create stunning sunsets because of particles in the air.**
- **Some plants and animals depend on wildfires to survive and thrive.**
- **Native Americans used controlled burns to manage forests and grasslands.**
- **Wildfires can reveal buried seeds, allowing rare plants to grow.**
- **Grasslands recover more quickly from wildfires than forests.**
- **Wildfires can destroy ancient trees that are hundreds or thousands of years old.**
- **People who live near forests often have evacuation plans for wildfires.**
- **Wildfire seasons are getting longer in many parts of the world.**

- Firebreaks made by bulldozers help stop wildfires from spreading.
- Airplanes called "super scoopers" drop thousands of gallons of water on wildfires.
- Firefighters sometimes dig trenches to stop wildfires from advancing.
- Wildfires can leave behind fertile soil that helps plants grow back.
- Some animals, like woodpeckers, make homes in burned trees.
- Wildfires teach us about the balance of nature and the importance of safety.
- Staying informed and prepared helps people stay safe during wildfire season.
- Learning about wildfires helps us understand how to protect the environment.

HEATWAVES

- A heatwave is a period of unusually high temperatures that lasts for several days.
- Heatwaves occur when temperatures are much hotter than normal for a specific area.
- Heatwaves can happen in any season but are most common in summer.
- Heatwaves are caused by high-pressure systems trapping heat in one area.
- During a heatwave, the air becomes still, and heat cannot escape.
- Heatwaves can happen anywhere in the world, including cold regions.
- Urban areas experience more heatwaves due to the urban heat island effect.
- The urban heat island effect occurs when cities trap heat in buildings and pavement.
- Heatwaves are more dangerous when combined with high humidity.

- High humidity makes it harder for sweat to cool the body.
- The heat index measures how hot it feels, combining temperature and humidity.
- A heatwave can cause dehydration if people don't drink enough water.
- Heatwaves can lead to heat exhaustion and heatstroke.
- Heat exhaustion can cause dizziness, headaches, and sweating.
- Heatstroke is very dangerous and happens when the body overheats.
- People should stay indoors and cool during a heatwave.
- Fans, air conditioning, and staying in the shade can help keep you cool.
- Wearing lightweight, light-colored clothing helps during a heatwave.

- Drinking plenty of water is the best way to stay hydrated in a heatwave.
- Heatwaves can cause power outages due to increased electricity use.
- Heatwaves are one of the deadliest weather events in the world.
- The hottest heatwave on record occurred in Death Valley, California, in 1913.
- Temperatures during that heatwave reached 134°F (57°C).
- Animals are also affected by heatwaves and may seek water and shade.
- Heatwaves can dry out soil and harm crops, causing food shortages.
- Droughts often accompany heatwaves, making water scarce.
- Forests and grasslands are more likely to catch fire during heatwaves.

- Heatwaves can cause roads to buckle and train tracks to bend.
- Many plants wilt or die during prolonged heatwaves.
- Heatwaves can harm fish by raising water temperatures in rivers and lakes.
- Heatwaves can cause health problems for pets, too.
- Dogs and cats need cool, shady places and plenty of water during heatwaves.
- Birds often cool off by splashing in water or hiding in trees.
- Zoos sometimes give animals frozen treats during heatwaves.
- Polar bears, penguins, and other cold-weather animals are especially vulnerable.
- Heatwaves can create smog by trapping air

pollution near the ground.
- Smog during heatwaves can cause breathing problems for people and animals.
- Kids can stay cool during a heatwave by playing in water or staying indoors.
- Many people use sprinklers or pools to cool off during a heatwave.
- Ice cream and popsicles are popular treats during hot weather.
- Heatwaves can lead to more insect activity, like mosquitoes and flies.
- Wild animals may come closer to towns and cities during heatwaves to find water.
- Cacti and desert plants are adapted to survive heatwaves.
- Some animals, like lizards, seek shade or burrow underground to escape heat.
- Birds often open their beaks to cool down

during heatwaves.
- Heatwaves can melt glaciers and speed up climate change.
- Airplanes sometimes can't take off during heatwaves because the air is too thin.
- Heatwaves can damage electronics and cause overheating in machines.
- People should avoid exercising outdoors during the hottest part of the day.
- Staying in cool places like libraries or shopping malls helps during a heatwave.
- Cities may set up cooling centers for people without air conditioning.
- Heatwaves can harm elderly people and young children the most.
- People can plant trees in their yards to create shade for future heatwaves.
- Heatwaves can cause headaches, fatigue,

and irritability in people.
- Wearing hats and sunglasses protects against sunburn during a heatwave.
- Heatwaves can affect animals in the wild and on farms.
- Cows, sheep, and other farm animals need extra water and shade during heatwaves.
- Some deserts, like the Sahara, experience heatwaves almost every day.
- Heatwaves are becoming more frequent and severe due to climate change.
- Global warming increases the likelihood of extreme heat events.
- The hottest temperature ever recorded on Earth was 136°F (58°C) in Libya.
- Drinking sports drinks can help replace salts lost through sweating in a heatwave.
- Trees and plants cool the air by releasing

water vapor, helping reduce heat.
• Air pollution can be worse during heatwaves because hot air traps pollutants.
• People can protect themselves by listening to weather reports during a heatwave.
• Solar panels produce more energy during heatwaves because of sunny skies.
• Heatwaves can cause flowers and plants to bloom earlier than usual.
• Staying informed about heatwave safety helps protect people and animals.
• After a heatwave ends, cooler weather feels even better!

HURRICANES

- A hurricane is a giant storm with strong winds and heavy rain.
- Hurricanes form over warm ocean waters near the equator.
- Hurricanes are also called typhoons or cyclones, depending on where they occur.
- In the Atlantic and Eastern Pacific, they are called hurricanes.
- In the Western Pacific, they are called typhoons.
- In the Indian Ocean and South Pacific, they are called cyclones.
- Hurricanes need warm water, moist air, and strong winds to form.
- A hurricane's center is called the eye, where it is calm and clear.
- Surrounding the eye is the eye wall, where the strongest winds and rain are found.

- Hurricanes are made up of spiraling clouds and thunderstorms.
- Hurricanes are classified on the Saffir-Simpson Hurricane Wind Scale.
- The scale ranges from Category 1 (weakest) to Category 5 (strongest).
- Category 5 hurricanes have wind speeds of over 157 mph.
- The strongest hurricane on record is Hurricane Patricia in 2015, with winds of 215 mph.
- Hurricanes can last for days or even weeks.
- Hurricanes can be hundreds of miles wide.
- Hurricanes spin counterclockwise in the Northern Hemisphere.
- In the Southern Hemisphere, hurricanes spin clockwise.
- The spinning motion of hurricanes is

caused by the Coriolis effect.
- Hurricane season runs from June to November in the Atlantic Ocean.
- The peak of hurricane season is in September.
- Hurricanes are tracked by meteorologists using satellites and radar.
- Special airplanes called Hurricane Hunters fly into hurricanes to collect data.
- Hurricanes can produce massive waves called storm surges.
- A storm surge is a rise in sea level caused by a hurricane's winds pushing water ashore
- Storm surges are the most dangerous part of a hurricane for coastal areas.
- Hurricanes bring heavy rain that can cause flooding.
- Hurricanes can create tornadoes as they

move over land.
- Hurricanes weaken when they move over land or cooler water.
- The word "hurricane" comes from Huracan, a Caribbean god of storms.
- Hurricanes are named using a list of names chosen by the World Meteorological Organization.
- Each year, names alternate between male and female.
- If a hurricane is very destructive, its name is retired and never used again.
- Hurricanes can damage homes, roads, and bridges with strong winds.
- Flying debris during hurricanes can cause injuries and damage.
- Hurricanes can knock down trees and power lines, causing blackouts.

- People prepare for hurricanes by boarding up windows and stocking supplies.
- Evacuating to a safe place is important during strong hurricanes.
- Some people build hurricane-resistant homes in hurricane-prone areas.
- Hurricanes can travel thousands of miles across the ocean.
- The path of a hurricane is called its track.
- Hurricanes often slow down and lose strength as they move inland.
- Hurricanes can cause landslides in mountainous areas.
- Flooding from hurricanes can take weeks to recede.
- The largest hurricane ever recorded was Hurricane Sandy, which was 1,150 miles wide.

- Hurricanes can make sea turtles lay their eggs earlier or later.
- Hurricanes help regulate Earth's temperature by moving heat from the tropics.
- Coral reefs can be damaged by hurricanes but often recover.
- Fish and other sea animals sometimes move to deeper water during hurricanes.
- Hurricanes can help spread seeds and bring new plants to islands.
- Animals like birds often fly away or find shelter before a hurricane hits.
- After a hurricane, ecosystems take time to recover, but nature is resilient.
- Hurricanes can wash away beaches and reshape coastlines.
- Scientists study hurricanes to improve

forecasting and safety measures.
- People can stay informed by listening to weather reports during hurricane season.
- Hurricanes are powerful, but they are also part of Earth's natural cycles.
- The Hurricane Belt is an area in the Atlantic Ocean where most hurricanes form.
- Hurricanes are most common in the Pacific and Atlantic Oceans.
- In 2005, Hurricane Katrina caused massive destruction in New Orleans.
- Hurricane Harvey in 2017 caused record-breaking flooding in Texas.
- The calm before the storm happens when the eye of the hurricane passes overhead.
- Hurricanes can carry rain and wind far inland, even to areas far from the coast.
- Some hurricanes move very slowly,

dumping lots of rain in one place.
- Fast-moving hurricanes can cause more wind damage but less flooding.
- Hurricanes form tropical depressions before becoming full-fledged storms.
- The average hurricane releases as much energy as 10,000 nuclear bombs.
- Hurricanes remind us of the power of nature and the importance of preparation.
- People plant mangroves and build levees to protect coasts from hurricane damage.
- Learning about hurricanes helps people stay safe and informed!

LANDSLIDES

- A landslide is when rocks, soil, or mud slide down a hill or mountain.
- Landslides can happen suddenly or over a long period.
- Landslides are caused by gravity pulling down loose material.
- Heavy rain is one of the most common causes of landslides.
- Earthquakes can also trigger landslides by shaking the ground.
- Volcanic eruptions can cause landslides by melting snow and ice.
- Landslides can be small or large, covering entire villages.
- Landslides can happen in forests, deserts, and mountains.
- Areas with steep slopes are more likely to have landslides.

- **Deforestation can increase the risk of landslides by removing tree roots that hold soil in place.**
- **Mudslides are a type of landslide with wet, flowing mud.**
- **Rockfalls are landslides with large rocks tumbling down a slope.**
- **Landslides often happen during or after heavy storms.**
- **Loose soil and broken rocks are called debris, and they make up most landslides.**
- **Landslides can block rivers, causing flooding upstream.**
- **Landslides under the ocean are called submarine landslides.**
- **Submarine landslides can trigger tsunamis.**
- **People living near cliffs or steep hills are more at risk for landslides.**

- Signs of a possible landslide include cracks in the ground or tilting trees.
- Landslides can destroy homes, roads, and bridges.
- Landslides are most common in hilly or mountainous regions.
- A landslide that moves quickly is called a rapid landslide.
- Slow-moving landslides are called creep and happen over time.
- Landslides can be as short as a few feet or stretch for miles.
- Planting trees and grass can help prevent landslides.
- Retaining walls and drainage systems also reduce landslide risk.
- Landslides can uncover fossils or buried artifacts.

- The largest landslide in recorded history happened in Alaska in 2015.
- Landslides can change the shape of the land, creating new hills or valleys.
- The energy of a landslide can move boulders weighing tons.
- Landslides can carry debris at speeds of over 100 miles per hour.
- Animals sometimes sense landslides before they happen and move to safer areas.
- Landslides often follow wildfires because burned areas have no vegetation to hold the soil.
- Mining and construction can increase the risk of landslides.
- Landslides are studied by scientists called geologists.
- Geologists use sensors and satellites to

monitor areas at risk for landslides.
- Landslides can happen on other planets, like Mars.
- Landslides on Mars are caused by dust and rocks shifting on steep slopes.
- Large landslides can create natural dams, blocking rivers.
- Landslides can bury roads and make it hard for emergency workers to help.
- Mud from landslides can stick to everything and take weeks to clean up.
- Landslides are part of Earth's natural process of reshaping the land.
- Many landslides occur during spring when snow melts and saturates the ground.
- Landslides can cause avalanches in snowy areas.
- Some landslides are triggered by human

activities like quarrying and deforestation.
- Landslides can create loud rumbling noises as they move downhill.
- The term "landslide" is often used to describe a big win in elections, but its original meaning is about moving earth.
- Heavy machinery is often needed to clear landslide debris.
- Landslides can move entire trees and toss them far away.
- In 1980, Mount St. Helens in the U.S. experienced a massive landslide during its eruption.
- Landslides can create new habitats for plants and animals.
- Grass and flowers often grow back quickly after a landslide.
- Some animals, like mountain goats, are

adapted to live in landslide-prone areas.
- Roads in landslide areas often have warning signs for falling rocks.
- Landslides can happen underwater, creating large waves or tsunamis.
- The Himalayas, Andes, and Rockies are mountain ranges prone to landslides.
- Landslides are less common in flat areas but can still occur during floods.
- Early warning systems can help save lives in landslide-prone regions.
- Landslides can create small hills or mounds called earthflows.
- Mudflows are faster than other types of landslides because they contain water.
- Landslides can make areas unsafe for farming and construction.
- Rebuilding after a landslide can take

months or years.
- Scientists study landslides to understand how to prevent them.
- Landslides remind us of the power of nature and the importance of safety.
- People living in landslide-prone areas should know evacuation routes.
- Learning about landslides helps us prepare and stay safe when they occur!

NATURAL DISASTERS IN HISTORY

Earthquakes

- The 2004 Indian Ocean Earthquake triggered a tsunami that killed over 230,000 people across 14 countries.
- The Great Kanto Earthquake in Japan (1923) killed over 140,000 people.
- In 1556, the Shaanxi Earthquake in China killed an estimated 830,000 people, making it the deadliest earthquake in history.
- The San Francisco Earthquake of 1906 destroyed much of the city with fires following the quake.
- The Haiti Earthquake in 2010 killed over 220,000 people and left millions homeless.
- The Lisbon Earthquake of 1755 caused tsunamis and fires, destroying much of the city.
- The Mexico City Earthquake in 1985 caused

widespread destruction and killed over 10,000 people.

Tsunamis

- The 2004 Indian Ocean Tsunami was one of the deadliest natural disasters ever.
- The 2011 Japan Tsunami caused massive destruction and a nuclear meltdown in Fukushima.
- The Krakatoa Eruption Tsunami in 1883 killed over 36,000 people in Indonesia.
- The Lisbon Tsunami of 1755 was caused by an earthquake and devastated Portugal's coast.
- The Tohoku Tsunami in 869 AD wiped out towns in ancient Japan.

In 1958, a tsunami in Alaska's Lituya Bay created a wave over 1,720 feet tall.

Volcanic Eruptions

- The eruption of Mount Vesuvius in AD 79 buried the Roman cities of Pompeii and Herculaneum.
- The Mount Tambora Eruption in 1815 caused "The Year Without a Summer," killing 71,000 people.
- The Krakatoa Eruption in 1883 created a global temperature drop and massive tsunamis.
- The eruption of Mount Pinatubo in the Philippines in 1991 lowered global temperatures for years.
- The Icelandic Laki Eruption in 1783 caused a famine that killed 25% of Iceland's population.
- The Mount St. Helens Eruption in 1980 was

the deadliest eruption in U.S. history.
• The Eyjafjallajökull Eruption in 2010 disrupted air travel across Europe for weeks.

Hurricanes
• Hurricane Katrina in 2005 caused over 1,800 deaths and severe flooding in New Orleans.
• The Great Galveston Hurricane of 1900 killed an estimated 8,000 people in Texas.
• Hurricane Harvey in 2017 caused record-breaking flooding in Texas.
• Hurricane Sandy in 2012 was the second costliest hurricane in U.S. history.
• Hurricane Maria in 2017 devastated Puerto Rico, causing thousands of deaths.
• The Bhola Cyclone of 1970 killed over 500,000 people in Bangladesh.

- Hurricane Andrew in 1992 was one of the most destructive storms in U.S. history.

Floods
- The China Floods of 1931 killed an estimated 4 million people, making it the deadliest flood in history.
- The Mississippi River Flood of 1927 displaced hundreds of thousands of people.
- The Pakistan Floods of 2010 affected 20 million people.
- The Netherlands North Sea Flood in 1953 killed over 1,800 people.
- The Yellow River Flood in 1887 killed nearly 900,000 people in China.
- The Johnstown Flood of 1889 killed over 2,200 people in Pennsylvania.
- The Kerala Floods in 2018 affected millions

in India.

Wildfires

- The Peshtigo Fire in 1871 killed over 1,500 people in Wisconsin and Michigan.
- The Great Chicago Fire in 1871 burned much of the city and killed 300 people.
- The Camp Fire in 2018 destroyed the town of Paradise, California, killing 85 people.
- The Black Saturday Bushfires in Australia (2009) killed 173 people.
- The Yellowstone Fires of 1988 burned 36% of Yellowstone National Park.
- The Mendocino Complex Fire in 2018 was California's largest wildfire in recorded history.
- The Greek Wildfires of 2007 killed 84 people and caused extensive damage.

Tornadoes

- The Tri-State Tornado in 1925 killed 695 people, the deadliest in U.S. history.
- The Joplin Tornado in 2011 killed 158 people and caused $2.8 billion in damages.
- The Daulatpur-Saturia Tornado in Bangladesh (1989) killed over 1,300 people.
- The Greensburg Tornado in 2007 destroyed 95% of the town in Kansas.
- The Moore Tornado in 2013 had winds of 210 mph, killing 24 people in Oklahoma.
- The Waco Tornado in 1953 killed 114 people in Texas.
- The El Reno Tornado in 2013 was the widest tornado ever recorded at 2.6 miles.

Blizzards

- The Great Blizzard of 1888 killed over 400 people in the U.S. Northeast.
- The Schoolhouse Blizzard of 1888 in the Midwest stranded children in schools, killing 235 people.
- The Iran Blizzard in 1972 killed 4,000 people, the deadliest on record.
- The Knickerbocker Storm in 1922 caused a theater roof to collapse in Washington, D.C.
- The Buffalo Blizzard of 1977 buried cars and houses under snowdrifts.
- The Siberian Snowstorm of 1966 was one of the coldest in history.
- The Blizzard of 1993, known as the "Storm of the Century," affected 26 U.S. states.

Heatwaves

The European Heatwave of 2003 killed over

- 70,000 people.
- The Chicago Heatwave of 1995 killed over 700 people in five days.
- The Indian Heatwave of 2015 killed over 2,500 people.
- The Pakistan Heatwave of 2015 killed over 1,200 people.
- The Australian Heatwave of 2009 caused deadly bushfires.
- The Phoenix Heatwave in 1990 reached 122°F, the hottest in Arizona history.
- The Moscow Heatwave in 2010 killed 56,000 people and caused wildfires.

Printed in Great Britain
by Amazon